796.357   Howell, Brian
HOW   New York Yankees

20%			
JA 2 7 '16			
MY 10			
SE 1 6 '12			
OC SE 9 '11			
OC 2 7			
NOV 0 3 2017			

NEW YORK
YANKEES

by Brian Howell

SportsZone
An Imprint of Abdo Publishing
www.abdopublishing.com

www.abdopublishing.com

Published by Abdo Publishing, a division of ABDO, PO Box 398166, Minneapolis, Minnesota 55439. Copyright © 2015 by Abdo Consulting Group, Inc. International copyrights reserved in all countries. No part of this book may be reproduced in any form without written permission from the publisher. SportsZone™ is a trademark and logo of Abdo Publishing.

Printed in the United States of America, North Mankato, Minnesota
052014
092014

Editor: Matt Tustison
Copy Editor: Nicholas Cafarelli
Interior Design and Production: Carol Castro
Cover Design: Kazuko Collins

Photo Credits: Paul Sancya/AP Images, cover; AP Images, title, 8, 11, 12, 17, 18, 20, 23, 26, 42 (top and middle), 44; Photo Mark Rucker/Transcendental Graphics/Getty Images, 4; Library of Congress/AP Images, 7, 14; File/AP Images, 25, 42 (bottom), 43 (top); Olen Collection/Diamond Images/Getty Images, 29; Focus On Sport/Getty Images, 30; Bill Janscha/AP Images, 33; Kathy Willens/AP Images, 34, 43 (middle); Eric Draper/AP Images, 37; Linda Kaye/AP Images, 39; David J. Phillip/AP Images, 41, 43 (bottom); Seth Wenig/AP Images, 47

Library of Congress Control Number: 2014933058
Cataloging-in-Publication Data
Howell, Brian, 1974.
  New York Yankees / by Brian Howell.
     p. cm. — (Inside MLB)
  Includes bibliographical references and index.
  ISBN 978-1-62403-478-7
  1. New York Yankees (Baseball team)—History—Juvenile literature. I. Title.
  GV875.N4H686 2015
  796.357'64097471—dc23

                    2014933058

TABLE OF CONTENTS

CHAPTER 1

THE BABE

Throughout the history of baseball, there have been many great players. There is one, however, who might stand above them all. Even many baseball fans who never saw him play believe he is the greatest to ever put on a uniform.

George Herman "Babe" Ruth was a home-run king and a winner of multiple World Series titles. The Hall of Famer was a hero to American sports fans in the 1920s and 1930s and is a legendary figure even today. And more than anyone else, he was responsible for making the New York Yankees the most famous team in professional sports.

"He was the one, the first one, the biggest one to bring recognition to the sport and make it what it has become today," said Cal Ripken Jr., a Hall of Fame player with the

The Yankees' Babe Ruth swings during batting practice in 1923. Many baseball experts still consider Ruth, who hit 714 career home runs, the greatest player in the sport's history.

Baltimore Orioles from 1981 to 2001.

Ruth, simply known as Babe, grew up in Baltimore, Maryland. He was a difficult child for his parents. So, at the age of seven, he was sent to St. Mary's Industrial School for Boys. It was there that he grew up. Although he had a tough childhood, Babe always loved baseball, and he was always a star on his team.

"Even as a kid I was big for my age, and because of my size I used to get most any job I liked on the team," he said. "Sometimes I pitched. Sometimes I caught. And frequently I played in the outfield and infield. It was all the same to me. All I wanted was to play."

Ruth signed his first professional contract as a teenager. He played his first major league game, with the Boston Red Sox, at the age of 19. By the time he was 20, he was already a major league star. Today, Ruth is known for the legendary home runs he hit when he played for the Yankees. But when he began his major league career, he was a dominant pitcher for the Red Sox. He had an 89–46 record for Boston.

With Ruth as one of their best players, the Red Sox won

Babe Celebrates

In the early 1900s, baseball players did not make as much money as they do now. But when Babe Ruth was 19 and he signed his first pro contract with the minor league Baltimore Orioles, he knew what to do with the money. "I went out and celebrated, just as soon as I got my first paycheck—$100. I bought a bicycle, something that I had wanted and often prayed for through most of my young life. Most of the Orioles, of course, had cars, but none of them was as proud as I was, riding the first possession of my life through the old streets of Baltimore," he said. Babe signed that contract in 1914.

Babe Ruth poses in 1919 while with the Red Sox. With Boston, Ruth was mainly a pitcher from 1914 to 1918 before becoming primarily an outfielder in 1919. After that season, he was sold to the Yankees for $125,000.

the World Series in 1915, 1916, and 1918. At that time, Ruth was one of the team's top pitchers, so he did not get to bat in every game. In fact, compared to his teammates, he hardly ever came to the plate. Still, he led the Red Sox in home runs in 1915, 1916, and 1918. Home runs were hard to come by in those days. But Ruth had 11 in 1918, leading all of baseball.

Because of his powerful bat, Red Sox manager Ed Barrow thought Ruth might be better suited to playing in the outfield instead of pitching. "The Babe agreed to play the outfield

Yankees star Babe Ruth talks to a group of children in 1924, telling them about his life and passing on his love for baseball.

"A Big Kid"

Babe Ruth loved kids more than any other group of fans he had. He spent hours signing autographs for children. He also often visited kids in hospitals. There are countless photos of Ruth surrounded by young fans. "Babe's love of kids was sincere. In many ways, he was a big kid himself," sportswriter Grantland Rice wrote.

principally, I think, because it got him into the game daily," Barrow said. Ruth became an outfielder in 1919. That season, he set a major league record for home runs in one season by hitting 29.

After the 1919 season, Ruth demanded that the Red Sox pay him more money. The

Red Sox refused, and owner Harry Frazee decided to sell Ruth for $125,000 to the rival Yankees. The impact of that deal would be felt for years. After winning the World Series three times with Ruth, the Red Sox went 86 years without another title. The Yankees, meanwhile, had never won a World Series before obtaining Ruth. Through 2013, they had won 27. This included the four they won with Ruth on the team.

After breaking the single-season home-run record in 1919 with 29, Ruth had 54 in 1920—his first season with the Yankees—and 59 in 1921. He did even better than that in 1927, when he hit 60—a record that stood for 34 years. Ruth, whose nicknames included "The Bambino" and "The Sultan of Swat," wound up hitting 659 home runs in 15 seasons with the Yankees. When he retired, he had 714 for his career. That number stood as the major league record until 1974.

Ruth was also a part of one of the greatest teams in baseball history. During his time in New York, the Yankees went to the World Series seven times, winning four of those Series. The 1927 team was considered to be possibly the best ever. That year, the Yankees went 110–44 during the regular season.

The 1927 Yankees had one of the best offensive teams in baseball history. Their lineup was so good that it was nicknamed "Murderer's Row." It featured Ruth, who batted .356 with 60 homers and 164 runs batted in (RBIs). First baseman Lou Gehrig, who hit .373 with 47 homers and 175 RBIs, was also an exceptional player. Gehrig was named the Most Valuable Player (MVP) of the American League (AL) that season.

(Until 1930, the AL had a rule that previous winners could not win again. Ruth was the MVP in 1923 and, therefore, could not win in 1927.) Second baseman Tony Lazzeri (.309, 102 RBIs) and outfielders Bob Meusel (.337, 103 RBIs) and Earle Combs (.356, 64 RBIs) were also sensational that season.

Ruth, Gehrig, Combs, and Lazzeri all became Hall of Famers. So did pitchers Waite Hoyt and Herb Pennock. Hoyt won 22 games in 1927, and Pennock won 19.

The Yankees had no problem winning the AL pennant, finishing 19 games ahead of the second-place Philadelphia Athletics. In the World Series, the Yankees swept the Pittsburgh Pirates four games to none.

The 1927 Yankees had a great collection of stars. And, throughout the history of the team, the Yankees have often had great stars. Ruth was the brightest of them all. He was inducted into the first Baseball Hall of Fame class in 1936. Not bad for someone who grew up with a tough childhood in Baltimore.

"What I am, what I have, what I am going to leave behind me—all this I owe to the game of baseball, without which I would have come out of St. Mary's Industrial School in Baltimore as a tailor, and a pretty bad one, at that," Ruth said.

Babe Ruth, *middle*, is shown with teammates Tony Lazzeri, *left*, and Lou Gehrig in 1927. The 1927 Yankees are often mentioned as one of the best teams of all time.

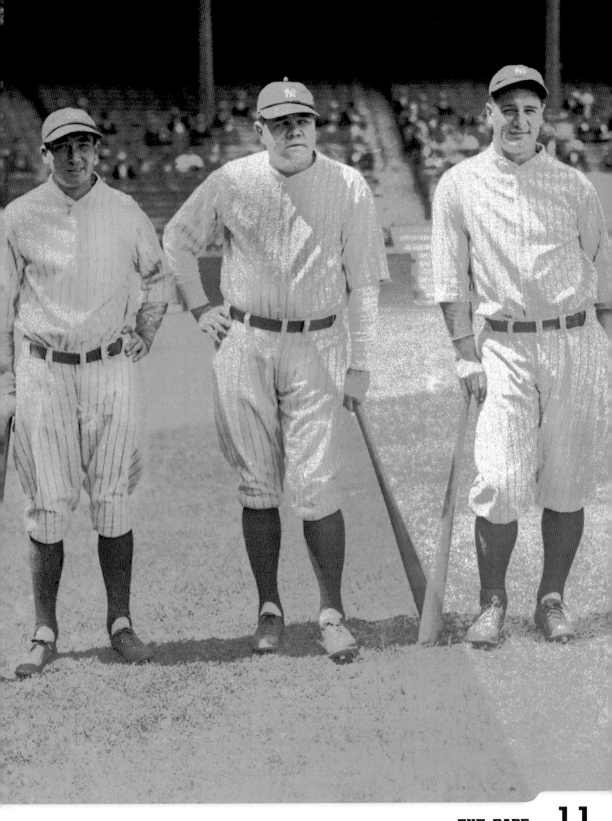

CHAPTER 2

GETTING STARTED

Today, the New York Yankees are one of the most popular sports teams in the world. But when the club was born in 1901, it was not located in New York. In fact, the team was not even called the Yankees.

Before 1901, the National League (NL) was the main league in professional baseball. One of the teams in the NL was the Baltimore Orioles, who played in the league from 1892 to 1899. At the end of the 1899 season, the NL decided to eliminate four teams. The Orioles were one of those teams. The manager of the Orioles was John McGraw, who was also a star third baseman.

When the NL eliminated the Orioles, McGraw and others were upset. A group of men led by Byron "Ban" Johnson and Charles Comiskey started a

John McGraw served as player/manager of the Baltimore Orioles when the team began play in 1901. The Orioles would move to New York and become the Highlanders and then the Yankees.

Pitcher Jack Chesbro won a record 41 games with the New York Highlanders in 1904. The Highlanders played from 1903 to 1912 before they were renamed the Yankees.

new league—the AL—in 1901. The group wanted to put a team in New York but could not since the NL already had two New York teams. So, they put a team in Baltimore and named it the Orioles. McGraw was named the team's manager. He was also a third baseman.

After two seasons, the AL and the NL ended their feud. The AL would be allowed to move a team into New York, so the Orioles packed their bags before the 1903 season.

In 1903, the team played its games at American League Park in New York. The field was located on one of the highest parts of Manhattan. Because of that, the park was referred to as Hilltop Park. The team took on the name of the Highlanders. They were known as the Highlanders for 10 seasons.

From the start, the Highlanders had great players. "Wee" Willie Keeler joined the Highlanders after spending four years with the Brooklyn team in the NL. The pitching staff in 1903 was led by Clark Griffith, who came from the Chicago White Sox, and Jack Chesbro and Jesse Tannehill, who both came from the Pittsburgh Pirates. Chesbro, Griffith, and Keeler all became Hall of Famers.

The Highlanders never did get to the World Series. They did finish second in the AL in 1904, 1906, and 1910. In 1904, Chesbro won 41 games, setting a modern record (since 1900).

In 1913, the team moved to the Polo Grounds, the New York Giants' home park. Moving away from Hilltop Park, the Highlanders changed their name. In 1913, they officially became known as the Yankees.

The franchise could not find a championship formula during its first 20 years. The team had some winning seasons. But it never could win the AL pennant and get to the World Series.

Life for the Yankees was changing, however. They hired manager Miller Huggins before the 1918 season. Huggins was a former big-league player who had managed the St. Louis Cardinals. Then, the biggest change came before the 1920 season. The Yankees purchased Babe Ruth from the Boston Red Sox. Ruth was a slugger who was about to change baseball, and the Yankees, forever.

The Yankees did not get to the World Series in 1920 either. But they won a team-record 95 games. Ruth was even better than expected, as he smashed 54 home runs. That season, the NL's Philadelphia Phillies were the only team to hit as many home runs as Ruth. The Phillies hit 64.

The 1920 season was just the beginning for Ruth and the Yankees. Ruth became the country's biggest baseball star. The Yankees, meanwhile, started making the postseason in 1921. The team won the AL pennant that year and the next but lost to the crosstown Giants both times in the World Series. The Yankees then broke through in 1923 with a World Series title, beating the Giants four games to two. Ruth hit three homers in the 1923 Series.

Before 1921, the Yankees had never been to the World Series. But in Ruth's 15 seasons (1920–34) with the team, New York won the AL pennant seven times and finished second five times. New York won the World Series in 1923, 1927, 1928, and 1932 in that period.

Of course, Ruth was not the only reason the Yankees were so good during those years. From 1925 to 1927, the Yankees had six future Hall of Famers on their roster. There were eight future Hall of Famers on the team in 1928 and as many as

Who Was Wally Pipp?

On June 2, 1925, Wally Pipp had a headache and could not play. So, rookie Lou Gehrig was put in the lineup. Pipp, who had been a regular in the lineup since 1915, never got his job back. "I took the two most expensive aspirins in history," Pipp said. Although best known for being replaced by Gehrig, Pipp was a standout player. He had a .281 lifetime batting average and twice led the AL in home runs.

Miller Huggins is shown in 1922. Huggins managed the Yankees from 1918 to 1929 and led the team to three World Series titles during that time.

nine during the early 1930s. Outfielder Earle Combs was one of them. He played for the team from 1924 to 1935. Others included catcher Bill Dickey (1928–43, 1946), infielder Tony Lazzeri (1926–37), and pitchers Herb Pennock (1923–33) and Waite Hoyt (1921–30).

If anyone on those Yankees teams could come close to Ruth in terms of talent, it was first baseman Lou Gehrig. Known as "The Iron Horse," Gehrig was a New York native. He is best known for two things—his remarkable streak of playing in 2,130 consecutive games, and the crippling disease that ended the streak and took his life in 1941. The streak was broken by the Baltimore Orioles'

Yankees legendary first baseman Lou Gehrig is shown in 1935. The Hall of Famer set a record by playing in 2,130 straight games from 1925 to 1939. The record was later broken by the Orioles' Cal Ripken Jr.

Cal Ripken Jr., who played in 2,632 straight games from 1982 to 1998. As of 2013, Gehrig and Ripken were the only players in MLB history to play in more than 1,307 straight games.

Amyotrophic lateral sclerosis (ALS), the neuromuscular disease with which Gehrig was diagnosed, eventually became known as Lou Gehrig's disease. A medical study released in 2010 suggested that concussions, or injuries to the brain, could contribute to ALS, or that there could be a separate condition that results from concussions and acts like ALS. During his career, Gehrig had several concussions that might have contributed to the disease that killed him.

Gehrig hit 493 home runs and drove in 1,995 runs during his career. He also compiled a .340 batting average. He was the AL's MVP twice, in 1927 and 1936. He played a significant role in six World Series title seasons for the Yankees. And he played in each of the first six All-Star Games in big-league history (1933–38).

With Ruth and Gehrig leading the way, the Yankees became a dominant team. But, as history would prove, that was just the beginning for the Yankees.

LUCKIEST MAN

Yankees star first baseman Lou Gehrig took himself out of the lineup on May 2, 1939, because he was ill. It was the first time in 14 years that he missed a game, but he would never play again.

On July 4, 1939, fans packed into Yankee Stadium for Lou Gehrig Appreciation Day. The Yankees retired Gehrig's No. 4, making him the first big-league player honored this way. Gehrig gave a famous speech. He began by saying, "Fans, for the past two weeks you have been reading about the bad break I got. Yet today I consider myself the luckiest man on the face of the Earth." And he ended with, "So I close in saying that I might have been given a bad break, but I've got an awful lot to live for."

Gehrig died on June 2, 1941, at age 37. The following day, flags flew at half-staff all over New York City and at baseball stadiums across the country.

CHAPTER 3

DOMINANCE

Just as Babe Ruth's time in New York was ending, the career of another great player was beginning. Ruth played his last season as a Yankee in 1934, at the age of 39. In 1936, 21-year-old Joe DiMaggio joined the Yankees' outfield.

Ruth was perhaps the greatest slugger of all time and became a national hero. DiMaggio just might be the greatest all-around baseball player ever, and he also became a hero. Like Ruth, DiMaggio was a larger-than-life figure who was loved around the country. He was not just a great baseball player; he also made news off the field. He left the Yankees during the middle of his career to join the Army, missing out on three seasons (1943–45). In 1954, he married the most famous woman in America at that time, actress Marilyn Monroe.

Center fielder Joe DiMaggio, shown in 1941, played for nine World Series title teams with the Yankees in his 13-year big-league career.

It was on the field where DiMaggio became famous, however. He was an outstanding hitter, fielder, and base runner. He finished his career with a .325 batting average. He also had 361 home runs and 1,537 RBIs. Those figures would have been higher had he not missed three seasons during the prime of his career for military service. His home stadium, Yankee Stadium, might have robbed him of some home runs too. Opening in 1923, the stadium was built with the left-handed hitting Ruth in mind. DiMaggio and other right-handed hitters had a tougher time hitting balls out.

DiMaggio made the AL All-Star team in each of his 13 seasons. He was the AL MVP in 1939, 1941, and 1947. He also holds one of the greatest records in baseball history, hitting in 56 consecutive games in 1941. As good as he was, DiMaggio was modest. "I'm just a ballplayer with one ambition, and that is to give it all I've got to help my ballclub win," he said.

When DiMaggio joined the team as a rookie in 1936, New York had not been to the World Series since 1932. The Yankees had plenty of talented players, such as catcher Bill Dickey, first baseman Lou Gehrig, and second baseman Tony Lazzeri. DiMaggio was the addition the Yankees needed.

One of a Kind

In 1946, the Yankees lost Hall of Fame catcher Bill Dickey to retirement. But that season, the Yankees also had 21-year-old catcher Yogi Berra. He also became a Hall of Famer, following a 19-year career. Berra was a three-time AL MVP (in 1951, 1954, and 1955), a 15-time All-Star, and a 10-time World Series champion. He has also become famous for his unique quotes, such as "A nickel ain't worth a dime anymore" and "It gets late early out there."

From left, Yankees stars Bill Dickey, Lou Gehrig, Joe DiMaggio, and Tony Lazzeri pose in 1936. The Yankees beat the New York Giants that year for the first of four straight World Series titles.

The core group of DiMaggio, Gehrig, Lazzeri, Red Rolfe, and George Selkirk, along with pitchers Red Ruffing, Lefty Gomez, and Monte Pearson, guided the Yankees to four consecutive World Series titles from 1936 to 1939.

In his 13 seasons, DiMaggio helped the Yankees reach the World Series 10 times. They won it nine times. New York also won a championship in 1943, when DiMaggio was away in the Army.

When DiMaggio retired after a 1951 World Series title win over the Giants, the Yankees did not have to look far for another star. DiMaggio's final season was also the first season for 19-year-old outfielder Mickey Mantle. Like Ruth and DiMaggio before him, Mantle was one of the greatest players of his era. During his 18-year career, he made the All-Star team 16 times. He was named the AL MVP three times, in 1956, 1957, and 1962.

Mantle finished his career with 536 home runs. Through 2013, he still had more home runs than any other switch-hitter in the game's history. "Mantle had more ability than any player I ever had on that club," said Casey Stengel, who managed the Yankees from 1949 to 1960.

As usual, Mantle was not the only great player the Yankees had. For much of Mantle's career, he played with one of the greatest catchers ever—Yogi Berra. Those Yankees teams also featured shortstop Phil Rizzuto and pitcher Whitey Ford, both Hall of Famers. The Yankees also had outfielder Roger Maris, a two-time AL MVP (1960 and 1961). Maris had one of the finest seasons ever in 1961, when he broke Ruth's home-run record of 60 in 1927 by hitting 61.

Led by Mantle, the Yankees continued to rule the AL. In Mantle's years, they went to the World Series 12 times, winning it seven times.

Perfection

Pitching a perfect game is one of the most difficult things to do in baseball. Doing it in the playoffs is even more difficult. The Yankees' Don Larsen accomplished the latter feat, however, pitching the first perfect game in postseason history. He did not allow any hits or any base runners in a 2–0 win over the visiting Brooklyn Dodgers in Game 5 of the 1956 World Series. "I was so weak in the knees out there in the ninth inning, I thought I was going to faint," he said.

The Yankees' Roger Maris, *left*, and Mickey Mantle are shown in 1961. Maris broke Babe Ruth's major league record with 61 homers that year, and Mantle hit 54.

Between the DiMaggio and Mantle eras, the Yankees strung together the greatest run in big-league history. During a 29-season stretch from 1936 to 1964, the Yankees were the AL champions 22 times. They also won 16 World Series championships in that time.

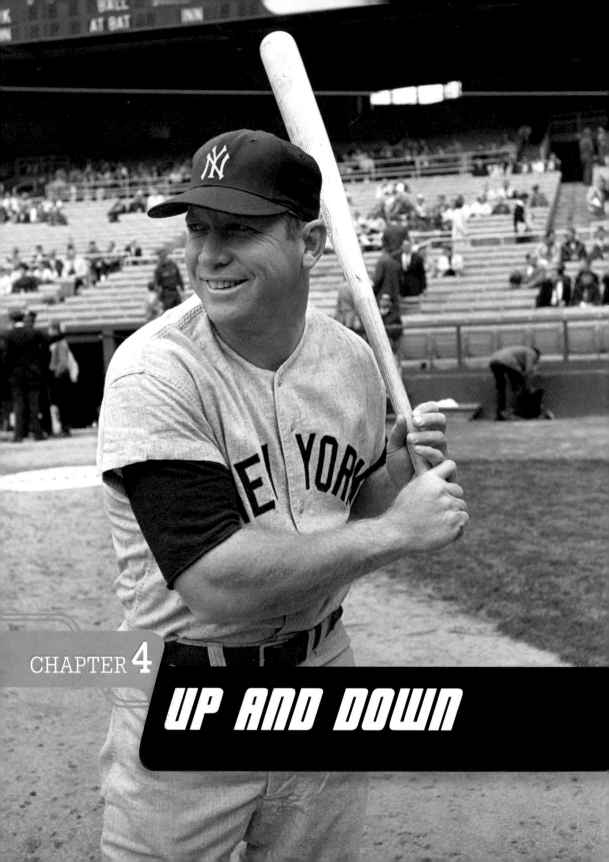

CHAPTER 4

UP AND DOWN

Even when the Yankees did not win World Series titles, they almost always were a good team. From 1919 to 1964, a stretch of 46 seasons, they had just one losing season—in 1925. They won 29 AL pennants and 20 World Series championships in those 46 seasons.

All that success made the 1965 season a weird one for the Yankees. They lost six of their first nine games and struggled all season. They finished 77–85, 25 games behind the first-place Minnesota Twins. That season, injuries took a toll on the Yankees. Mickey Mantle played most of the season. But he did so with pain in his knees and had his worst season.

Unlike other seasons when the Yankees failed to make the Series, 1965 signaled a more long-term problem. The Yankees had always had better players than everybody else.

Star slugger Mickey Mantle smiles for a photo in 1965, but he played in pain that season. The Yankees finished 77–85 and began a streak of 11 straight years in which they did not qualify for the postseason.

But now those players were older and injured. The Yankees also had always had better minor league players than anybody else.

The star power and depth of talent that made the Yankees great was gone in 1965. Suddenly, the Yankees were just an average team—for the first time in nearly five decades.

The Yankees were even worse in 1966, when they placed last in the AL. It was the first time the Yankees sank to the bottom of the league since 1912. Life did not get much easier in the following years either. In fact, after winning 99 games in 1964 and losing in the World Series in seven games to the St. Louis Cardinals, the Yankees missed the postseason in 11 straight years. It was their longest playoff drought since before Babe Ruth joined the team in 1920.

In 1973, the Yankees got the change they needed. George Steinbrenner, who worked for a shipbuilding company, led a group that purchased the Yankees for $10 million. "The Boss," as Steinbrenner became known, demanded excellence from his team. "I learned as a young man that discipline is needed in all athletes," Steinbrenner said in 1998. "I'm a disciplinarian."

The Yankees were an improved team in Steinbrenner's first three years as owner. In his fourth year, 1976, they finally got back to the postseason. They lost the World Series in four games against the Cincinnati Reds. Veteran catcher Thurman Munson was the AL's MVP that season. But it was several important moves off the field that helped build that team. In 1974, the Yankees traded for first baseman Chris Chambliss. In 1975,

George Steinbrenner answers questions in January 1973 after he became the Yankees' new owner. Team president Michael Burke is at left.

Steinbrenner made a splash by signing former Oakland Athletics pitcher Jim "Catfish" Hunter to a big free-agent contract. Before the 1976 season, the Yankees traded for second baseman Willie Randolph and outfielder Mickey Rivers. All of them became valuable members of the new-look Yankees, who found the 1976 season to be the start of another stretch of successful years.

In 1977, the Yankees added free-agent slugger Reggie Jackson and Ron Guidry became a regular member of the pitching staff. The core group from 1976 was still intact. Veteran third baseman Graig Nettles

Reggie Jackson bats during Game 6 of the 1977 World Series. "Mr. October" hit three home runs in the Yankees' 8–4 win over the Dodgers that wrapped up the title.

smashed a career-high 37 home runs in 1977. That same year, relief pitcher Sparky Lyle won the AL Cy Young Award. With so much talent on the roster, the Yankees had what it took to get back to the top. They won 100 games during the regular season and then defeated the Los Angeles Dodgers four games to two to win the World Series for the first time in 15 years.

One year later, in 1978, the Yankees did it again. They won 100 games during the regular season. Guidry, nicknamed "Louisiana Lightning," went

25–3 with a 1.74 earned-run average (ERA) and won the Cy Young Award. The team also received pitching contributions from Hunter and reliever Goose Gossage, both future Hall of Famers. The Yankees defeated the Dodgers in six games to win the World Series. That season is best remembered for New York's remarkable comeback, which was capped by one remarkable game.

On July 17, 1978, the Yankees sat in fourth place in the AL East, 14 games behind the first-place Boston Red Sox. Six days later, Yankees manager Billy Martin resigned. Bob Lemon, who had been let go as manager of the White Sox earlier that season, took over. The Yankees began catching up to the rival Red Sox. When the regular season ended, both teams were 99–63.

MR. OCTOBER

During the Yankees' title-clinching 8–4 win over the Dodgers in Game 6 of the 1977 World Series at Yankee Stadium, Reggie Jackson smacked three home runs, driving in five runs.

Jackson's star performance in that game was a big reason he was given the nickname "Mr. October." He received this nickname because the playoffs are played in October, and that was when Jackson was often at his best.

Jackson hit five homers in the 1977 World Series. In 34 postseason games as a Yankee, Jackson smashed 12 home runs. After helping the Oakland Athletics win three straight World Series from 1972 to 1974, he played a big role for the Yankees as they won back-to-back titles in 1977 and 1978.

So, they met on October 2 at Boston's Fenway Park for a one-game playoff to determine who would go to the postseason.

Boston led 2–0 going into the seventh inning. That is when an unlikely hero emerged. Shortstop Bucky Dent, who had just four home runs all year, hit a three-run shot just over the famed "Green Monster" left-field wall—the top portion of which is more than 30 feet off the ground. The shot gave the Yankees a 3–2 lead. New York held on to win 5–4 and earn a spot in the playoffs.

The Yankees remained a very good team for several more years. From 1976 to 1981, they made the playoffs five times and got to the World Series four times.

After losing the 1981 World Series in six games to the Dodgers, however, the Yankees went through another down period, by their standards. Although they produced seven winning seasons from 1982 to 1994, they did not qualify for the playoffs in any of those 13 years.

During that era, the Yankees had some great players. Future Hall of Famers Rickey Henderson and Dave Winfield, both outfielders, played for the team in that time. Another star for the Yankees during this period was first baseman Don

Gone Too Soon

At the heart of the Yankees during the 1970s was catcher Thurman Munson. He was named AL Rookie of the Year in 1970 and the league's MVP in 1976. He was having another strong season in 1979 when tragedy struck. On August 2, 1979, Munson was flying in his new jet when the jet crashed, taking Munson's life. "I don't know if we will ever recover from that death," Yankees owner George Steinbrenner said in 1998. "His locker is still in the locker room, and it will be there."

Don Mattingly is congratulated by third-base coach Mike Ferraro after hitting a home run in 1987.

Mattingly. The only time that he got to the playoffs was in his final season, in 1995. Of the 16 Yankees players to have their number retired by the team through 2013, Mattingly was the only one who never played in a World Series. The others all won at least one World Series. Mattingly came to the team after one great stretch of success. And his career ended just before another great stretch.

Donnie Baseball

The Yankees' Don Mattingly, nick-named "Donnie Baseball," made six straight All-Star teams from 1984 to 1989 and was named the AL's MVP in 1985. That year, Mattingly batted .324 with 35 homers and an AL-best 145 RBIs. He was also a great fielder, winning nine Gold Gloves for his work at first base. A back injury bothered him during the second half of his career. But he still finished his career with 2,153 hits and a lifetime batting average of .307 over parts of 14 seasons, all with the Yankees.

CHAPTER 5

RETURN TO DOMINANCE

Derek Jeter was a kid in Kalamazoo, Michigan, when he realized what he wanted to do with his life. "I was about eight years old as I walked along our thick carpet, past the pictures of my grandparents on the hallway walls and into my parents' bedroom," he said. "I announced that I was going to play for the Yankees."

Jeter never lost sight of that goal. In 1992, he was drafted by the Yankees. He signed a contract with the team one day after his 18th birthday. He was 20 years old when he played his first game in a Yankees uniform in 1995.

Also during that 1995 season, catcher Jorge Posada, starting pitcher Andy Pettitte, and relief pitcher Mariano Rivera made their major league debuts with the Yankees. Together with Jeter, those players formed the nucleus of

Derek Jeter celebrates during the 1996 playoffs. The rookie shortstop helped New York capture its first World Series title since 1978.

another Yankees dynasty for more than fifteen years.

With the help of their rookies, the Yankees got a taste of the playoffs in 1995 under manager Buck Showalter. New York made the postseason as the AL's wild-card team. The Yankees fell three games to two to the Seattle Mariners in the AL Division Series (ALDS). After that season, owner George Steinbrenner replaced Showalter with Joe Torre.

Jeter, Pettitte, Posada, and Rivera became full-time contributors in 1996. The youngsters teamed with veterans such as Tino Martinez, Paul O'Neill, and Bernie Williams to form a championship team. The Yankees finished 92–70 and won the AL East for the first time since 1981. They then won the World Series for the first time since 1978, beating the Atlanta Braves in six games.

The Yankees tend to win championships in bunches. This new group was no different. From 1995 to 2007, the Yankees went to the playoffs 13 years in a row. They had never done this previously. Of course, having the wild-card playoff position—which went into effect in 1995—helped. But the Yankees won their division 10 times in those years.

In 1998, the Yankees set a team record for wins, going 114–48. They then rolled through

Andy Pettitte pitches during Game 4 of the 1998 World Series. Pettitte threw 7 1/3 innings of shutout ball to help New York prevail 3–0 at San Diego and clinch the title.

the playoffs and swept the San Diego Padres in the World Series. The Yankees repeated as World Series champions in 1999, sweeping Atlanta. They then won the title again in 2000, defeating the crosstown New York Mets four games to one in the "Subway Series." The Yankees captured the last two of those crowns with the help of veteran pitcher Roger Clemens, whom they acquired before the 1999 season.

"Winning four World Series out of five years in this

day and age when you have to come through layer after layer of postseason play, we can put our record, our dedication, our resolve up against any team that's played the game, in my mind," Torre said after the 2000 World Series.

In 2004, the Yankees acquired Alex Rodriguez from Texas, sending second baseman Alfonso Soriano to the Rangers as part of the deal. Rodriguez made five All-Star teams and won two MVP Awards in his first five seasons with the Yankees. He had been a star shortstop with the Seattle Mariners and then Texas. But he became a third baseman with the Yankees because they already had Jeter at shortstop.

As good as the Yankees were, they never won another World Series after 2000 under Torre's direction. They continued to get to the playoffs every year through 2007. Torre departed after that season. New York lost a thrilling seven-game World Series to the Arizona Diamondbacks in 2001. Two years later, the Florida Marlins upset the Yankees in six games in the World Series.

Torre left to become the Los Angeles Dodgers' manager

Mo and Andy

Mariano Rivera was nearly unhittable as a relief pitcher. Andy Pettitte was one of the great big-game pitchers of all time. Together, they played major roles in keeping the Yankees among the elite teams in baseball. Through 2013, when Rivera left the Yankees, he had 652 regular-season saves during his 19 years in the big leagues, all with New York. In the postseason, the right-hander had a record 42 saves and 0.70 ERA. His "cut fastball" was a dominant pitch that hitters could rarely solve. Through 2013, the left-handed Pettitte had won 219 regular-season games and 18 more in the playoffs in his 15 years as a Yankee (1995–2003 and 2007–13).

Manager Joe Torre, *left*, and star third baseman Alex Rodriguez embrace in 2006. The two were together with the Yankees from 2004 to 2007, but the team did not win a World Series in that stretch.

starting with the 2008 season. His 12-year tenure managing the Yankees trailed only Joe McCarthy's 16 years (1931–46) running the team.

Joe Girardi, a former Yankees catcher, took over as manager in 2008. New York's run of playoff appearances came to a close. The Yankees won 89 games, but finished third in the mighty AL East.

In 2009, Girardi guided the Yankees back to the top. Led once again by Jeter, Pettitte, Posada, and Rivera, the Yankees won 103 regular-season games and beat the Philadelphia

STEINBRENNER PASSES AWAY

On the morning of July 13, 2010, longtime Yankees owner George Steinbrenner died after suffering a heart attack in Tampa, Florida. He was 80 years old.

Steinbrenner had been the Yankees' owner since 1973. His 37-year tenure as owner was the longest in team history. The Yankees won seven World Series and 11 AL pennants in the time that he was owner. His outspokenness and tendency to fire managers frequently bothered some people, but no one could argue his devotion to the Yankees.

On July 16, the Yankees paid tribute to "The Boss" with a 15-minute ceremony before their home game against the Tampa Bay Rays. The Yankees also honored Bob Sheppard at the ceremony. Sheppard, the distinctive public-address announcer at Yankee Stadium from 1951 to 2007, passed away two days before Steinbrenner. Sheppard was 99.

Phillies four games to two in the World Series. In addition to their four leaders, the Yankees also had Rodriguez and other stars such as second baseman Robinson Cano, first baseman Mark Teixeira, and starting pitcher CC Sabathia showing the way.

"It's awesome," Rivera said after the 2009 World Series win. "I never want to forget what it feels like to be right in there [in the celebration], to be the last team standing."

Led by the same core players, the Yankees returned again to the postseason in 2010. New York was the wild-card team this time after being edged out by the Tampa Bay Rays for the AL East title. Still, New York finished 95–67 and swept the Minnesota Twins in the ALDS. In the AL Championship Series (ALCS),

Shortstop Derek Jeter, *middle*, and closer Mariano Rivera smile in 2009 while looking at the World Series trophy the Yankees won by beating the Phillies in six games.

however, the upstart Texas Rangers won in six games.

The Yankees returned to the playoffs in 2011. However, they lost in five games to the Detroit Tigers. The Yankees advanced to the ALCS in 2012. But the Tigers swept the series, depriving the Yankees of a return trip to the World Series.

Then in 2013, the Yankees missed the playoffs for only the second time in 19 seasons.

Yet with 27 World Series crowns, the Yankees have often been the last team standing. With titles coming in bunches, it's difficult for anyone who follows the Yankees to ever forget the championship feeling.

TIMELINE

1901 The Baltimore Orioles, who would become the Yankees, begin play in 1901 in the AL, which formed that year.

1903 The Orioles move to New York and change their name to the Highlanders. In 1913, the team is renamed the Yankees.

1919 On December 26, the Boston Red Sox sell slugger Babe Ruth to the Yankees for $125,000. Ruth goes on to hit 659 home runs in 15 years with the Yankees. He helps them win four World Series titles.

1936 A year after Ruth retires, the Yankees have a new star in 21-year-old rookie Joe DiMaggio. The outfielder and veteran first baseman Lou Gehrig both have sensational seasons in leading the Yankees to the first of four straight World Series titles.

1941 In the regular season, DiMaggio sets a major league record with a 56-game hitting streak. New York wins the World Series again, for a ninth time. The Yankees defeat the Brooklyn Dodgers four games to one.

1953 Catcher Yogi Berra and 21-year-old outfielder Mickey Mantle guide the Yankees to the World Series championship for the fifth year in a row—a streak that still stands as the longest in baseball history. New York tops Brooklyn in six games.

1956 Don Larsen pitches a perfect game in Game 5 of the World Series against Brooklyn, lifting New York to a 2–0 home win on October 8. The Yankees win the Series in seven games.

1961	Roger Maris breaks Ruth's single-season home-run record with 61. New York beats the Cincinnati Reds in five games for its 19th World Series title.
1977	The Yankees defeat the Los Angeles Dodgers in six games for their first World Series title in 15 years. Reggie Jackson hits three home runs for New York in the clinching 8–4 home victory on October 18.
1978	The Yankees defeat the Dodgers again in six games for the World Series title.

1996	With rookie shortstop Derek Jeter helping lead the way, the Yankees climb back to the top again. They defeat the Atlanta Braves in six games for their 23rd championship and first since 1978.
2000	Manager Joe Torre guides his team to a third consecutive championship and the fourth in five years, as the Yankees defeat the New York Mets in five games in the World Series.
2007	The Yankees earn the AL wild-card spot with a 94–68 record. The Yankees fall three games to one to the Cleveland Indians in the ALDS. After the season, Torre leaves the Yankees, ending a 12-season tenure as manager.

2009	Back in the playoffs after a year away, the Yankees defeat the Philadelphia Phillies in six games in the World Series. It is the 27th World Series championship for the Yankees.
2013	After unsuccessful trips to the playoffs in 2011 and 2012, the Yankees miss a chance at the playoffs for just the second time in 19 seasons.

QUICK STATS

FRANCHISE HISTORY

Baltimore Orioles (1901–02)
New York Highlanders (1903–12)
New York Yankees (1913–)

WORLD SERIES
(wins in bold)

1921, 1922, **1923**, 1926, **1927**, **1928**,
1932, **1936**, **1937**, **1938**, **1939**, **1941**,
1942, **1943**, **1947**, **1949**, **1950**, **1951**,
1952, **1953**, 1955, **1956**, 1957, **1958**,
1960, **1961**, **1962**, 1963, 1964, 1976,
1977, **1978**, 1981, **1996**, **1998**, **1999**,
2000, 2001, 2003, **2009**

KEY PLAYERS
(position[s]; seasons with team)

Yogi Berra (C/OF; 1946–63)
Bill Dickey (C; 1928–43, 1946)
Joe DiMaggio (OF; 1936–42,
   1946–51)

Whitey Ford (SP; 1950, 1953–67)
Lou Gehrig (1B; 1923–39)
Reggie Jackson (OF/DH; 1977–81)
Derek Jeter (SS; 1995–)
Mickey Mantle (OF/1B; 1951–68)
Roger Maris (OF; 1960–66)
Don Mattingly (1B/OF; 1982–95)
Thurman Munson (C; 1969–79)
Mariano Rivera (RP; 1995–2013)
Alex Rodriguez (3B; 2004–)
Babe Ruth (OF/SP; 1920–34)

KEY MANAGERS

Miller Huggins (1918–29):
   1,067–719; 18–15–1 (postseason)
Joe McCarthy (1931–46):
   1,460–867; 29–9 (postseason)
Casey Stengel (1949–60):
   1,149–696; 37–26 (postseason)
Joe Torre (1996–2007):
   1,173–767; 76–47 (postseason)

HOME PARKS

Oriole Park (1901–02)
Hilltop Park (1903–12)
The Polo Grounds (1913–22)
Yankee Stadium (I) (1923–73,
   1976–2008)
Shea Stadium (1974–75)
Yankee Stadium (II) (2009–)

* All statistics through 2013 season

QUOTES AND ANECDOTES

Yankee Stadium originally opened in 1923. It became known as "the House that Ruth Built" because Babe Ruth's prime years as a player coincided with the stadium's opening and the beginning of the Yankees' success. After closing for two years for renovations, the famed ballpark reopened in 1976. Then, in 2009, a brand-new Yankee Stadium opened across the street from the old one. The new stadium included several design elements from the previous stadium, paying tribute to the team's rich history. But the new stadium also had all the amenities one would expect in a modern ballpark. One addition at the new ballpark is the Great Hall, a large concourse that is lined with banners of past and present Yankees stars. The reported final cost of the new stadium was a whopping $2.3 billion.

"Heroes are people who are all good with no bad in them. That's the way I always saw Joe DiMaggio. He was beyond question one of the greatest players of the century."
—Mickey Mantle, on fellow former Yankees great Joe DiMaggio

"Baseball is ninety percent mental. The other half is physical."
—Yankees Hall of Fame catcher Yogi Berra, known for his one-of-a-kind quotations

In 1973, the AL adopted the designated hitter rule, which allowed teams to put a better hitter in the lineup in place of the pitcher. The first man to appear in a game as a designated hitter was the Yankees' Ron Blomberg. He made his mark on history on April 6, 1973, when he walked with the bases loaded in his first plate appearance in New York's 15–5 loss to the host Boston Red Sox. He finished the game 1-for-3 with the RBI walk.

GLOSSARY

acquire

To add a player, usually through the draft, free agency, or a trade.

debut

To make a first appearance.

dynasty

A team that wins a lot of games, usually including more than one league championship, over a time spanning multiple seasons.

franchise

An entire sports organization, including the players, coaches, and staff.

free agent

A player whose contract has expired and who is able to sign with a team of his choice.

legendary

Well known and admired over a long period.

neuromuscular

Referring to the body's nerves and muscles.

pennant

A flag. In baseball, it symbolizes that a team has won its league championship.

rookie

A first-year player in the major leagues.

switch-hitter

A batter who can hit left-handed or right-handed.

tenure

A span of time that somebody is with a team.

wild card

Playoff berths given to the best remaining teams that did not win their respective divisions.

FOR MORE INFORMATION

Further Reading

Krantz, Les. *Yankee Stadium: A Tribute*. New York: It Books, 2008.

Miller, Ernestine. *The Babe Book*. Kansas City, MO: Andrews McMeel Publishing, 2000.

Vecsey, George. *Baseball: A History of America's Favorite Game*. New York: Modern Library, 2008.

Websites

To learn more about Inside MLB, visit **booklinks.abdopublishing.com**. These links are routinely monitored and updated to provide the most current information available.

Places to Visit

George M. Steinbrenner Field
One Steinbrenner Drive
Tampa, FL 33614
813-875-7753
www.steinbrennerfield.com
This has been the Yankees' spring-training ballpark since 1996. It is where the team plays its home games in preparation for the regular season.

**National Baseball
Hall of Fame and Museum**
25 Main Street
Cooperstown, NY 13326
888-HALL-OF-FAME
http://baseballhall.org
This hall of fame and museum highlights the greatest players and moments in the history of baseball. Babe Ruth, Lou Gehrig, and Joe DiMaggio are among the former Yankees enshrined here.

Yankee Stadium
One East 161st Street
Bronx, NY 10451
718-293-4300
mlb.mlb.com/nyy/ballpark/index.jsp
The new Yankee Stadium has been the Yankees' home field since 2009. The team plays 81 regular-season games here each year.

INDEX

About the Author

Brian Howell is a freelance writer based in Denver, Colorado. He has covered the Denver Broncos for the past three years for the *Longmont Times-Call* and covered the Colorado Rockies during the 2007 and 2008 seasons. He has earned several writing awards during his career. He lives with his wife and four children.